How to Improve Your Golf Game (And Your Life!)

Learn the secret ways that winners think.

How to improve your golf game (and your life!)

How to Improve Your Golf Game (And Your Life!)

Learn the secret ways that winners think.

By Ed McCosh

Beyond Expectations Publishing

Acknowledgements

As always I'm eternally grateful to my Mum and Dad and my brother David for all their love and support. Thanks to Judymay Murphy too for helping me come up with the idea for this book.

I'd also like to say a big thank you to all the people I've worked with who have sent me notes and emails thanking me. It's incredibly rewarding to hear about your progress and I thank you for taking a moment to tell me.

How to improve your golf game (and your life!)

Contents

Introduction   **1**

Develop a winning mindset   **4**
   Being realistic   6
   Placing your order   9
   Managing expectations   12
   Maintaining a streak   16
   "But I haven't done it before…"   19
   Are you playing not to lose?   20
   "Who do you think will win?"   25
   "But I don't know how"   30
   Pre game visualisation   33
   No limits   36
   Which shot are you playing?   42
   Use weighted dice   45
   Take control of your emotions   49
   The irony of anger   53
   Be more emotional   56

During the round   **60**

Releasing physical tension   **62**
     Breathing to relax   69
     Breathing to get yourself motivated   72
     Push the button   75
Psychology   **81**
     Let go of nerves…   81
     …or be a butterfly collector   83
     You are a magnet   84
     Garbage in, garbage out   91
     Ask a silly question…   95
Enjoying yourself more   **99**
     Living in the future   99
     You don't hit the ball with your head   103
     Putting it all together   109
Practicing   **117**
     Don't be crazy!   117
     Review what you've learned   119

How to improve your golf game (and your life!)

How to improve your golf game (and your life!)

Introduction

Have you ever experienced the frustration of hitting the ball better in practice than you do on the course? Do you find it hard to keep a hot streak going or maintain a lead? Are you unsure about how hard to hit putts? Perhaps you feel your game isn't getting better despite the fact you are practicing harder?

There is a common theme in all of these things. It's not the technical part of your swing – after all if you're hitting the ball well at the range or during a hot streak on the course, then you have a swing that works! That means that your thoughts are undermining your swing.

You only have to look at how the top players prepare. Ernie Els and Retief Goosen have both said that mental coaching work was vital in helping them become Majors winners. Arnold Palmer said that the game was 90% mental and Tiger Woods has admitted that his Dad helped him develop his mental toughness.

That's where this book comes in. It's full of simple tips that will help you make changes to the way you think to improve your scores.

You may have heard the claim that you can tell a lot about a person by the way they play a sport. Perhaps this is because life itself is just a game. You might decide to look at the way you play golf, to see where you can improve your life. With that in mind there is an extra bonus at the end of each chapter that will show you how you can apply these tips to the rest of your life too!

Develop a winning mindset

It's important to begin seeing things differently before you even get to the practice range or course. This section provides you with the foundations of the winning mindset that will help you on the course.

Be careful not to fall into the trap of making generalisations. Sometimes you might hear something familiar and say 'yes, yes I know that'. Don't assume that doing something similar to the tips here is enough. There are subtle differences in the way that winners think and behave. Be honest with yourself about whether you are really doing these things consistently.

You will build on the tips in this section later in the book, so do the short exercises as you come to them. They won't take long, but it is amazing how often not now, becomes never.

Being realistic

Let's start with what you want to achieve. How much better are you going to get? When? Are your goals exciting enough to motivate you to take action? If you don't set goals to be better, then the likelihood is that you won't get better. You need to be clear about what you want to accomplish.

Challenge your perceptions of how good you think you can be. Did you know that OJ Simpson (the actor and American Football player) had rickets and wore braces on his legs until the age of five? But OJ had a goal that he was determined achieve and he went on to become a record breaker in the all time Hall of Fame. So set ambitious goals, not just what you think is 'realistic'.

Don't use your previous shots as the basis for what you can do. They are in the past and if you only look at what you have done as a guide to what you can do, then it's likely that you'll keep producing same shots!

How this applies to your life

In what areas are you limiting your success by basing what you can do in the future by what you've done in the past? Remember that you can do more than you think.

Placing your order

You need to write down your goals of how you want to play, what you want to win, and perhaps even how you want to feel. Don't just keep them in your head. Why? You are taking in millions of bits of information per second on an unconscious level; but you can only consciously cope with hundreds of bits per second. So it's important to make it clear what you want your mind to focus on. Think of it like a waiter taking your order and keeping it in his head. He then goes to the kitchen and tells the chef, who also keeps the order in his head. After several orders it becomes very difficult to remember what you asked for.

So write down your goals now - and be specific. "I want to improve my handicap" isn't as effective as "I am improving my handicap by 2 shots by a certain date". Putting a deadline on your goal will motivate you to start working out what steps you'll take to make it happen - now rather than later. Please also notice that you want to write your goals as though you are achieving them now or as though you've done them already; that is unless you want them to stay out of reach in the future?

How this applies to your life

Do you plan what you want to happen in your life?

Or are you just leaving it to chance? Write down goals for other areas of your life too. What kind of lifestyle do you want? What is your partner like? What level of health do you want? What are your career goals?

Managing expectations

A note of caution about writing goals before a round. At this point don't set yourself a target score. This will either put pressure on you not to hit any bad shots if it is a low score, or lead to you being sloppy if it is a score that seems easy to you.

One thing I've noticed is that golfers of all abilities often start out with the aim of not hitting any bad shots in a round. You may well be sitting there thinking "Er, yes that's the hope!"

However, think about it. No golfer has ever hit the ball exactly where he wants it to go, exactly the way he wanted to, on every shot during a round. Yet how often do we hear people (including ourselves) being self critical when we mishit a shot?

Think about the pressure this aim puts on you. Again it comes back to the fact that if your expectations are too high, it's almost a relief to hit a bad shot as the pressure is released. Remember that Tiger Woods hits bad shots. It's not about never hitting bad shots; it's about reacting positively to them and minimising the damage they do.

So instead set yourself goals relating to controlling your emotions. For example, decide to remain calm if shots don't go just the way you hoped, not to judge them at all (even just to yourself!) and to focus on the things that you're good at.

How this applies to your life

It's fine to decide what you want to happen, but it's important to recognise that you can't control everything. Don't give up if (when) things don't always go the way you hoped; instead adjust your expectations to allow for occasional setbacks and attach less significance to them. You can also increase your chances of success by focusing on the things that you can control, such as your emotions. Decide to pay attention to the energy that you give out. Are you going to be a positive person who attracts success, or a negative one who drives it away?

Maintaining a streak

You know those times when you start playing well for several holes and you start to believe that you are playing above yourself (based on your usual score - in the past). When you are under this illusion, you are out of your comfort zone. As you have a natural human need to feel secure, you end up taking action to change the situation... and you blow it. You are disappointed, but at the same time you feel a great relief, as you're back on familiar ground.

The way to avoid this is to spend time imagining yourself playing at this new level before you get to the course. Picture the shots you'll hit, see your score card, hear others comments about how well you're playing, and imagine how you'll feel. This process helps you to become used to this situation (your unconscious doesn't know the difference between you imagining this and it actually happening), so when it does happen, it feels normal. Take as long as you need just now to add these details to the goals you wrote down earlier.

How this applies to your life

Again you need to imagine yourself living the life that you want to. How will you behave, what will you do? What changes do you need to make to get where you want to be?

You may find this process easier if you think of someone that you admire and imagine how they would deal with different situations. Then all you need to do is copy them!

"But I haven't done it before..."

Sometimes we find it hard to imagine ourselves doing dramatically better than we are. But how little would you achieve in life if you only did things that you'd done before? Think of a time when you did something that you'd never done before. Did you tell yourself that you couldn't do it, or did you decide what you wanted and then try to do it? Remember the old line that there's always a first time!

Are you playing not to lose?

Sometimes when we are playing well or even before we start, our hope is that we "Don't blow it!" Many of our bad shots and lost leads come from our attempts not to blow it or 'not to lose'. When your focus is on protecting yourself, you become defensive. This means that you are physically tighter, that your thoughts are less clear and the quality of your decisions is reduced. Think about it; you don't make your best decisions when you are fearful. How often have you come up short with approach shots or putts because you didn't want to go through the green? When you focus on 'not messing it up' that is often precisely what happens.

The key is to focus on playing to win. If you're beating your opponent, then your aim is to get further ahead (not to maintain your position). In life we either grow or whither. Which would you prefer? If you find yourself being fearful about what could go wrong with a shot then stop what you are doing and start again. If you try to hit the ball with this kind of thinking your chances of hitting a good shot are slim. You need to play with conviction. This means getting yourself into a positive physical position and frame of mind, and focusing on what you want to happen.

"The key to superior play is to be in a resourceful state of mind (rather than survival mode!)"

This is not about being reckless and going for every pin. Sometimes the best shot might be to 'play safe' in the middle of the green. But it's important that you get yourself into a state where you make decisions about the shot calmly and commit to it completely. When it comes to the shot, rather than thinking to yourself "Ok, I don't want to go into that bunker, so I'd better be careful and go for the centre", you need to say "The easiest place to hit it is the centre of the green, look at all the space there" or something similar.

It's a subtle, but crucial difference and I'll explain why in the chapter titled "You are a magnet."

How this applies to your life

Are there other areas in your life where you are playing not to lose? Perhaps you are interested in taking a course that will benefit you, but you are focusing on keeping the money that you have, rather than how you can invest it to make it go further. Or are you trying to stay safe in an ever shrinking comfort zone, by putting off a call that could make a difference, because you don't know what the outcome will be? If so, get yourself into a confident state and remind yourself of what you want to happen – then go for it.

"Who do you think will win?"

I'm always amazed when I hear players tell journalists that they think someone else will win the tournament they're about to play in. They are already putting the person they are tipping above them, meaning that they have to do something special to beat this person. Sometimes their egos are such that they actually want to lose to that person – so they can say they were right!

You have to begin with the belief that you are the best player in the competition until the final standings say differently. Leave it to other people to prove if they are better than you on that day.

Sometimes people are uncomfortable about this. They don't want to publicly set themselves up for a fall. Admittedly announcing to the world that you believe you are going to win the tournament could definitely lead to extra pressure on you. But be aware of the difference between arrogance and confidence. Of course you don't want to come across as arrogant; and there is a difference between saying "I'm definitely better than everyone else" (arrogance) and "I'm good at this and I'm in with as good a chance as anyone else" (healthy self belief).

A top football player recently told me why his manager was able to get him and his team mates to consistently punch above their weight. He explained that all week the manager gave the players subtle encouragement in training, then before the match he'd really talk them up so their belief was sky high! It reminded me that the best way to get the best from someone is through encouragement; try it on yourself!

You may still want to keep your beliefs about who you think will win to yourself, but make sure that YOU see yourself as the main contender.

How this applies to your life

How often do you put other people on a pedestal, where you pretend that they have more experience, more skill, or better looks etc than you? It's time to start seeing yourself as someone unique who has just as much potential as anyone else. The people you look up to are not fundamentally different to you physically or mentally – they are just taking different actions to you. To some people it seems incredibly difficult to lose weight, whilst others would say "It's easy; you just do this, this and this". There are so many examples of people who have overcome incredible adversity to achieve their dreams, and it's not that they were super human beings. They are normal human beings like you and I, but they have decided to take super human actions.

"But I don't know how"

It's easy to talk yourself out of something, especially if you focus on how you're going to do it. When something is in the future there are endless possibilities about how it might turn out. So if you try to work out every scenario before you take action, then a) you're going to be there for a while, and b) you're likely to find lots of reasons why you can't do it.

Rather than focusing on how you're going to do something, concentrate on what you want to happen. I remember a bunker shot I had which looked impossible. The ball was at the back of the bunker, very close to the lip, so my swing was very restricted. To make it harder the pin was only a few feet beyond the other end of the bunker, on a fast green. And I was playing in a competition! The guys I was playing with were full of helpful comments, including "Let's see how you're going to deal with that"; I had no idea! All I could do was focus on what I wanted to happen and trust that I'd find a way; and to my delight and their surprise the ball ended up a foot away from the hole.

How this applies to your life

There are many times when we are held back because we aren't sure how to do something. The thing to remember is that we learn best by doing. Sometimes we have lots of reasons why we can't do something, when all we need is one reason why we can! If you have a good enough reason why you want to do something, then you'll find a way to make it happen. You don't need to see every step – just the next one.

Pre game visualisation

So here's the next step you're going to take to improve your game. If you look into how people achieve amazing feats, they nearly always mention visualisation. They talk about the mental preparation they did before hand, and that they pictured every step they would take.

Many of the golfing greats also say that they picture their round before they play. So imagine how you want to play the night before a game. Go through every shot and see yourself as composed, calm and confident. Although we can all do it with different degrees of ease, some people believe that they can't make pictures in their head. It might be that you find it easier to imagine the sounds or feelings that you will have as you play. Just do whatever is easiest for you. You can even hold the club if it helps!

How this applies to your life

You probably already rehearse how things will go in your head. It might just be a case of being more conscious that you can use this as a technique to help you prepare for something, and to make sure that you imagine yourself doing whatever it is successfully!

No limits

The biggest obstacle to our success occurs when we don't believe that we can achieve something. Nearly everyone I've worked with has had a limiting belief of some sort about what they can achieve.

Examples of limiting beliefs include:
- I can't hit this shot / club
- I never get a good score on this hole
- I can't play well for a full round
- I always blow it

- I can't help getting angry

Put simply they are different forms of 'I'm not good enough to do 'x'.

Sometimes they can be more subtle such as:

- "It's a relief to get my first bad shot / hole out of the way" (in other words I believe I'm definitely going to hit one ball out of bounds!)

Write down your beliefs about your own golf game. In what ways are you living with limitations?

It's important to realise that you are more than the labels that you attach to yourself. Your handicap can be limiting, as part of you aims to play to it, rather than under it. Remember that you probably had a higher handicap before, but then one day you scored lower; so you can do it again anytime you play. Realise that you've hit good shots with every club a number of times – so it's possible for you to hit the shots required for a great score.

Be aware of your limiting beliefs and be sure to ignore them if they pop up. Focus on times when you have done something well instead and anything else that helps you feel more positive.

How this applies to your life

You can achieve so much more than you think. The most common limiting belief is "I'm not good enough", which leads to most of our stress and anxiety. You know the times when you feel like something intangible is holding you back from your full potential? The chances are that it's because of this belief. When there is an action you want to take, but don't take, it's likely that it's because of this belief. Please don't feel bad if you recognise that this belief has affected you before – it's a universal fear. However, it is important to realise that this is a ridiculous belief that undermines your ambitions and enjoyment of life. Since it is at the root of all fear, it's a major topic and my book *"Am I good enough?"* will help you break its hold over you on a deeper level of consciousness, so you really feel different.

Every moment is an opportunity to create a new reality for yourself. What happened in the past is in the past and set backs are not due to some intrinsic part of you that can't be changed. It's not like the moment you were born, people pointed and said "Look – a nervous baby!" We are only acting in certain ways. So start taking action to become who you want to be. For example, if you want to be more confident then act in a confident way. Soon it'll seem like normal behaviour to you.

Which shot are you playing?

This is a good time to ask yourself how often you have spoiled your current shot by replaying a previous poor shot in your head. Remember that the shot you are on now is physically unconnected to previous ones. Even on a day when your swing isn't where you want it to be, it's probably only a millimetre or two away from clicking. It might not feel like it, but even if you have just hit a series of poor shots, the next shot can be fantastic.

We often expect things to happen due to what has happened in the past; we become conditioned to expect good or bad things. For example, when you are a hoping that a good run won't end (because that has happened before). Remember that the future *is* unknown and that every moment is an opportunity to create a new reality.

How this applies to your life

The same principles relate to the rest of your life. People often give up just as they are on the verge of success. Keep going – things will turn around and you're probably much closer to reaching your goal than you think.

Be willing to redefine yourself in a positive way every day - or even every moment. Decide to be unstoppable today!

Use weighted dice

There is an approach that allows you to think about the past in a beneficial way. Focusing on the things that you've done well in the past for example! You might be thinking, 'Hang on, you've just said that the past isn't linked to the future', which is true; but great players move the goal posts depending on the situation in order to make it easier for them to succeed.

It's as though their attitude is determined by weighted dice that are always in their favour.

If it isn't helpful to think about a certain shot they don't; whilst if it will help them they do. They keep adjusting their focus so that it is on the things they do well.

Let's say that they have missed a few putts. Some people might decide that they weren't getting the breaks today. Players with a great mental attitude decide that the law of averages means that they are more likely to get one because of the misses.

At the same time, if they sink a few putts, they don't think 'Well, according to the law of averages, I'll probably miss some soon'. They think "Wow, I'm really on form today, I'm going to get even more in!"

They choose to see every experience in a positive light. If they repeatedly lose a lead they don't decide that they are likely to choke under pressure. They see each loss as experience that is helping them become accustomed to the pressures of being in front.

How this applies to your life

You can choose how you interpret the events in your life. Take the case of two of my friends who had a very negative upbringing. Their father was always quick to say that things couldn't be done and was unhappy having achieved very little with his own life. One son moped around and followed in his father's footsteps, but the other had incredible determination and achieved great success. When I asked why their life had turned out that way they both responded in the same way:

"How else could I be, with a father like that?"

Take control of your emotions

Building on the previous point, it's important that you accept that you are the only person who decides your thoughts and feelings. No person or thing makes you feel anything – your feelings start within you and are therefore things that you create. This applies to all emotions, but we'll focus on anger, as golf can certainly seem like a frustrating sport.

First of all you don't 'have to' get angry. You choose to feel angry because you don't like something. You know this is important. If you lose control of your emotions when you're playing golf then your score can - and often will - be spoiled very quickly. And there are lots of potential distractions in golf. Other players talking. Planes overhead. The weather (especially in Scotland!) Dog walkers. Having to wait for slow play, or feeling like you have to rush your shot when playing through. The actual occurrence of these things is out with your control. For many of us this is a source of great frustration; we like control! So what can you control?

The one thing that you can control is your response to events. If you find yourself saying "It made me" or "I can't help it" about anything or anyone, on and off the golf course, then correct yourself. It might take some practice, but you can develop new ways of responding to things. We are creatures of habit, so develop healthy habits that benefit you. Give things a different meaning like the example in the previous chapter, or choose to let them go. Things can only bother you if you resist them. Your anger will not improve your game and it probably won't even stop whatever you thought was irritating you. This isn't to say that you won't ever feel anger again. The point is that you have the choice about whether you want to become angrier about it, or let it go.

The irony of anger

The number one aim of your unconscious mind is to maintain your health. On a golf course there is very little that will actually physically harm you, but your angry comes from situations when you tell yourself that something is threatening you. Your unconscious mind probably pretends that getting angry helps because you can feel powerful. It does not help! The ironic thing is that by becoming angry you are harming yourself; as becoming angry for a few minutes results in a decrease in the immune system for several hours.

Getting uptight about things is a bit less tempting isn't it?

The other downside of reacting angrily is that your playing partners won't enjoy being around you as much. Many people worry that other people won't like them if they don't play well enough. But who would you rather play with? An unfriendly tense low handicapper (not that all low handicappers are like this at all!) or a friendly, fun high handicapper.

If you start to feel angry, take a deep breath and breathe out the tension. That way you are not suppressing it, merely releasing it in a healthier way. You can also learn much more to help you make healthier choices over anger in my book *"Letting go of anger."*

Be more emotional

Have you ever told someone about a very funny comedian you saw, but found that you couldn't remember any of their jokes? We don't always remember what people said, but we remember how they made us feel. This is because:

a) We have to find a way to manage huge amounts of information, so it is easier to generalise about situations, than it is to remember the details.

b) Everything we do is driven by our desire to feel a certain way. We do things for emotional reasons, not intellectual ones.

So we are conditioned to remember situations where we have experienced strong emotions, but we do so in a generalised way.

In golfing terms this means that you want to be selective about how you react to your shots. If you react angrily to a missed putt, then it will stay in your mind for much longer than if you accept it. So when I say be more emotional I'm talking about more positive emotions. Reserve your emotional moments for the good shots that you want more of! You know those short putts that you expect yourself to get, but occasionally miss? Generally we become angry when we miss them and brood about them for the next few holes, but we hardly ever remember them when they go in. Rather than getting upset about the misses, start celebrating the ones you get – even on the putting green. This will help to build up a good feeling around them and you'll miss a lot less.

How this applies to your life

What things in your life are you treating like those short putts that you expect to make? What little things you could be more relaxed about? What could you celebrate more? For example, sometimes we take waking up each day for granted. Lots of people say that their health is the most important thing; but they are most aware of it when they are ill. Start being grateful for it every day and enjoying all the things you have now.

During the round

The way that you choose to cope with your emotions has a very significant outcome on your success as a golfer. Take Colin Montgomerie's mishit 7-iron on the 18th that cost him the Open at Winged Foot. Did Colin mishit a shot from the fairway because he wasn't technically good enough? Of course not. The tension of the moment got to him.

Tension causes bad shots and this tension is caused by uncertainty and self imposed pressure without the correct release.

In this section you're going to learn how to deal with tension and manage your emotions.

Releasing physical tension

The starting point for coping with emotions such as anxiety, disappointment and anger is how you use your body. People often try to think their way out of situations. Or to put it another way, if they are feeling negative, they try to 'think' of a solution. The problem is that this isn't how the human body works. In order to change your emotional psychology you actually have to change your physiology. If you don't do the right things physically, it's very hard to change the way you feel. Put simply the way you use your body can make things better or worse.

Colin Montgomerie and Tiger Woods demonstrate this perfectly. When things are going wrong for Monty his body language becomes defeatist. He waits tensely, with clenched jaw before shots, then his shoulders slump forward and his head hangs in despair afterwards. In contrast Tiger's body language is a great example. As he walks down the fairway his posture is upright, with his shoulders back, head up, and chest pushed out making for a very purposeful stride. Sometimes when the pressure is on you can even see a subtle, but unmistakeable moment where Tiger raises his game. He raises his chest just a little higher and struts with even more determination and purpose, leading to commentators saying things like "Here comes Tiger!"

Here's how to use your body in the most effective ways to send positive messages to your mind.

Firstly, before you pick up a club, relax your shoulders and make sure that hands are unclenched. Don't clamp your jaw together either. A tightening of the muscles, dipping your head and closing your jaw tight (both to prevent concussion) are all natural reactions – if you need to protect yourself in a fight. Now I know golf can be competitive, but the effects of these actions won't help your game. Firstly, if your muscles are tight you will actually lose distance. Your arm is moved by a series of opposing muscles (which are complex enough; it takes 72 co-operative muscles just to speak.) Therefore, in order for them to be at their most effective you want to be as relaxed as possible. Furthermore, when you get tense you are sending an unconscious message to your body telling it to prepare for a threat. It responds by releasing adrenalin. A little adrenalin can help, but too much will give you that shaky feeling in your hands and running at this higher level puts a greater strain on your body. So even if your thoughts are anxious, make an effort to relax your body.

Begin by relaxing your hands and shoulders, and keeping your chin up! You want to look straight ahead, because you use certain parts of the brain depending where you look with your eyes. All you're doing is going along with the way that your body works. It's not a coincidence that when someone feels confident and happy they look up, whilst when someone is anxious or sad they look down. So if you think being confident and happy will be better for your game then keep your head and eye line up.

Stand as though your feet are planted into the ground with deep roots, so that you feel steady and secure in your body. Move deliberately, with purpose.

Remember that image of Tiger marching down the fairways? You can use the same positive energy in your game by raising your breastbone. Stand up straight now with your head up, shoulders back and then just lift up your chest just a little more, as though it's being pulled upwards. Notice how much more assertive and in control you look (and guess what message you're sending to your unconscious?)

Breathing to relax

Breathing is one of the most powerful ways to release tension about a shot. When you are tense it's likely that your breath is short and limited to the top part of your lungs, and that you suck in your stomach when you take a deep breath. Breathing like this pulls the diaphragm up, which reduces the space for your lungs to inflate.

Instead breathe in slowly and deeply through your nose, and imagine the air being channelled down your back and inflating your stomach. Take a moment or two now to get the hang of this. It often helps to rest your hand on your stomach, so you can check that it is inflating and coming out, rather than going in as you breathe in. What you're doing here makes your diaphragm go down, so your lungs can fully inflate.

Breathe out steadily through your open mouth (this will stop you clenching your jaw) with a quiet 'ha' sound until you have nothing left to exhale. Notice how you feel calmer and a tension has shifted from your chest.

Before you begin your round do 20 minutes of this kind of breathing. (You might want to start with 5 minutes and quickly build up; since it feels pretty good, you'll want to do more.) You can do it in your car on the way to the course. If you begin to feel nervous at any point, just start breathing this way. Do it on every shot and practice your pre-shot routine so that your swing begins immediately after you have finished exhaling.

This is one of the most natural and healthy ways to feel good, and there's an unlimited, free supply any time you want it – so enjoy it!

Breathing to get yourself motivated

Alternatively you can also use a slightly different breathing method to get yourself more 'pumped up' if necessary. Sometimes I've found myself standing at the first tee on a cold morning and not really felt like I was physically ready to begin. So I take a few sharp strong breaths in through my nose and then breathe out a few times through my mouth (as though I'm trying to blow out a candle). After a few minutes of this kind of breathing you'll feel dramatically different. Stronger, more alert and more focused. If you find yourself in a similar situation where you need to get yourself going, then you can use this technique.

So in summary:

- Relax your hands and shoulders
- Lift your chin up and look straight ahead
- Plant your feet firmly in the ground
- Move purposefully
- Raise your chest up
- Breathe effectively

How this applies to your life

Whenever you want to perform at your best or make an important decision – even if it's just about what club to choose, or how hard to hit a putt - you want to be in a positive frame of mind. Decisions that are based on fear are rarely the best option available to you. Use these techniques to get yourself into a confident state, then assess your options. The breathing techniques in particular will also help you remain calm if you have to speak in public, or if you want to be alert but relaxed whilst in traffic.

Push the button

A big part of hitting a good shot is feeling confident about it. So here's how you can feel calm and confident at will. When you hear certain songs you are reminded of a positive memory that makes you feel good. This is an example of something external (the sound) creating an internal response in you. You can use something similar to create an invisible button on your body that makes you feel confident when pressed. Then if you want to feel confident – for example, on the first tee – all you have to do is press your button!

Follow these simple steps to set your button up now.

Setting up your confidence button:

1. Choose where you want the button to be. I'd recommend your 4th knuckle on the hand that is nearest to the club head in your golf grip. That way you can press it easily with your index finger before a shot.

2. Relax and remember a time that you felt supremely confident (it can be about any activity). Allow yourself to go back to that time, see what you saw then through your eyes and really take on the same feelings. Take as long as you need to really get into the feeling again now.

3. When the feeling is at its strongest point, apply pressure to your knuckle. Maintain the pressure until the feeling starts to subside; at this point take your finger off your knuckle.

4. Shake your hand out, then repeat steps 2 & 3 for other positive emotions, such as being calm, happy, determined, focused and strong. Do these one at a time on the same knuckle, with the same pressure as before, shaking your hand out between each emotion.

5. Now press the same knuckle and all your previous positive feelings will return. Feels pretty good, right!

You've set up your confidence button and instant confidence is at your fingertips! You can follow the steps above and keep adding positive emotions, so that it becomes even stronger.

You can use it for other activities in life where you want to feel more confident too.

How this applies to your life

It's much easier to change your thoughts after you have changed your physical state. The next section teaches you how to deal with negative thoughts when you're on the course.

Psychology

Let go of nerves...

Here is a very simple mental technique that you can use with your confidence button, if you are feeling nervous about a shot.

1. As always begin by standing in a confident way.

2. Imagine yourself a few minutes ahead in your future, after you have successfully completed the shot. Make a note of how the shot looked or felt, including the sound of the club striking it, or the sound of it dropping into the hole. Enjoy the experience.

3. Realise how calm you feel about the shot once you've imagined that it's gone well. Play your shot.

...or be a butterfly collector

If there are ever still a few butterflies there then embrace them! They are a sign that you are where you are supposed to be and part of the excitement!

Similarly if you are playing well and people start saying "you're going to win", use this as a way to remind you to focus on every shot (you'll learn more about this in "Putting it all together".) Remember nothing has changed; you are the one who got yourself into a good position, so you can continue to play well.

You are a magnet

Many studies have shown that our thoughts are the deciding factor on whether we succeed or fail. This chapter is really important. It's about making sure that you choose thoughts that attract the results you want.

How many times have you told yourself 'not to lift your head', 'not to swing too fast', 'not to leave it short', 'not to go into the bunker', only for precisely that thing to happen? There is a reason for this - and it's not that you're dumb or lacking concentration! It's just that you gave your mind the wrong instructions.

You need to understand two key things about your mind that will change your golf game:

1. Your unconscious mind (the control centre that decides what to focus on) doesn't pay attention to the word 'not'.

2. Your thoughts are magnetic.

This means that you attract whatever you focus on regardless of whether you believe that it is good or bad.

Give it a try. Don't think of one your favourite songs or TV programmes. Let me guess – it just popped into your head? Oops! You can keep trying not to think about it, but what you'll find is that you probably end up adding more details about it.

Applying this to golf is simple, yet powerful. Instead of telling yourself 'not' to do certain things, focus on where you want the ball to go. For example, "Don't hit it into that greenside bunker", becomes "Hit it into the heart of the green."

Another common experience is getting nervous when someone is watching you. Rather than praying that you don't make a mess of it in front of them, get excited by the opportunity to show them what you can do and inspire them.

This isn't about never having any more negative thoughts, as this is unlikely – you're not a robot and emotions are natural. It's just about being more aware of your thoughts and repeating positive ones to yourself instead. It's ok if you are aware of some negative thoughts; the positive ones are hundreds of times more powerful.

Throughout this book I've been emphasising the importance of writing things down, as it's easier for your mind to remember exactly what you want and also because otherwise we tend to switch to autopilot. The aim of our mind's autopilot mode is to protect us, so we look out for things we want to avoid. Writing down the positive things you want to happen will help you take control back from the autopilot system, so that your mind knows to look for positive things.

Go back to the goals you wrote down earlier about what you're going to achieve. It can take a little practice to change habits, so start now by ensuring that your goals are about what you want to happen (i.e. "I want to get more putts", rather than "I want to miss less.") This also applies to the way you want to feel, which I'm guessing is confident and calm, rather than anxious or tense.

How this applies to your life

Where you have been aiming in other parts of your life? Constantly check that you are working at what you want to happen, not what you don't want to happen and you'll achieve a lot more.

Garbage in, garbage out

Earlier we mentioned the benefit of encouraging yourself. You also want to cut out insults to yourself such as "You idiot, you messed up." You didn't do it intentionally and I've yet to see a player who improved his concentration by becoming frustrated with himself. Do you think you have more chance of hitting a good shot when you feel good about yourself or when you've just been told that you're a useless underperformer?

Start to become aware of how you describe your round or how you're feeling. When someone asks 'How are you?' one of the most common responses is 'Not bad.' Given what you just learned about the how the mind relates to the word 'not', you might want to change this to 'ok', 'good' or even 'great!' You might just start believing it!

Tiger tends to find a way to see his game in a positive light; in interviews he may mention an area he wants to improve or work on, but at the same time he'll say he was pretty pleased about some aspect of his game. However disappointed you are with your game, always find a way to take a positive from the round. If there is a part you want to improve, then say that "it could be better", rather than "it was terrible." You're building feeling and momentum for your game – in which direction do you want it to be?

How this applies to your life

Practise being positive and looking for areas where you're doing well in other aspects of life too. For a start, if you spend all week being negative, you'll find it hard to be positive for a game of golf at the weekend!

Ask a silly question...

Your mind loves to answer questions – doesn't it?

This can be a great problem solving tool; the only problem is that we often ask ourselves unhelpful questions! For example, we often say "Why can't I stop doing this?" Do you really want to know why you can't stop doing it? Or would a question like "How I am going to change things now?" be more helpful? Remember that your mind will try to answer whatever you ask it.

Avoid the question 'Why did I do that?' when you are on the course*. The reason you'd ask this, is because you want to figure out what went wrong and avoid it next time. However, when you've just hit a poor shot, you are not in the most resourceful state. But your mind still wants to answer the question, so you'll get a string of negative ideas that are linked to your state.

*Save any work on your swing for the practice range. Even then don't react to every mishit shot. You'll just start over correcting and creating problems where they didn't occur. If you are experiencing the same problem consistently, then you can consider 'what can I do differently?' Keep technical work for the range and when you're on the course accept the way you are swinging on the day.

If you are unsure of which club to play, which line to choose or how hard to hit a putt, simply say to yourself say "Ok and if I did know what would it be....?" Then stick with your gut feeling.

How this applies to your life

Use questions to change the way you deal with situations. You don't need to eradicate all negative questions from your life; just increase your awareness of them, so that you can change them. For example, when you wake up in the morning, rather than asking "Why am I so tired?" ask "How would I feel if I felt wide awake?" It might sound simple, but it makes a difference to how you feel.

Enjoying yourself more

Living in the future

It was clear to one of my teachers that we couldn't wait to finish the last couple of months at school. Thankfully, he was a smart guy and he made a very intelligent point that has stayed with me since then. He asked when we were going to relax? Once the school exams were finished? Or once university exams were complete? Or would it be after we retired?

Even if your livelihood is linked to your golf game, your true aim in playing is to feel good, because this is the ultimate aim behind every activity. Therefore look for ways to enjoy the experience, regardless of the weather or your score. Otherwise when are you going to start enjoying your golf? Next time? What if there wasn't a next time? It's important to enjoy things now and being grateful for the opportunity to play is a great start.

People often say that they'll enjoy themselves more when they play well. In reality it's the other way around. When you are more relaxed, you will play better golf.

How this applies to your life

My book *"Am I good enough?"* disproves one of the great myths in our society, which is that we have to do or have certain things in order to feel good. There is nothing that you should do; only the things that you want to do.

Remember the breathing technique we went through earlier. It feels good just to breathe and enjoy being. Don't 'wait' impatiently anymore. For example, if someone is playing more slowly than you on the golf course, instead of wanting them to play faster and feeling impatient, stop waiting and start enjoying where you are. Notice the things around you. Enjoy being.

This applies to waiting in traffic or in a queue at a shop. If you accept things as they are then you will feel better. You want the queue to go faster because you are busy. So be thankful for the chance to take a few moments to pause and relax in your otherwise hectic day.

You don't hit the ball with your head

I talk to people a lot about how getting more in touch with the unconscious part of their mind and body will help them. Let me explain what I mean by that. Your conscious mind relates to the things that you are very aware of, and you can associate it with being in your head. Your unconscious is the part of the mind that does things like beating your heart without you asking it to. With regard to golf let's imagine that it is located throughout your body. It operates with the conscious mind, but the unconscious is the one that's really in charge. It decides all of your behaviour, based on its number one objective, which is to preserve your health and happiness.

Why am I telling you this? Because you don't hit the ball with your head or conscious mind. You hit it with your body.

This means that you want to think less about how you swing the club. If you're making a change to your swing at the range, then at first you might be focusing on how you're drawing the club back and so on, but if you want to hit the ball with all of your potential, you need to let go. Your conscious mind can't keep up with the swing. Remember that the opposing muscles that move your arm are most effective when you are relaxed. When you try to think your way through a golf shot do you feel loose and fluid or tight and like you're forcing it? You need to trust that your unconscious knows how to hit the ball better than your conscious mind. You hit lots of physical targets unconsciously every day! When was the last time that you missed your mouth with your toothbrush?

Don't worry about any negative thoughts that you are conscious of. Rather than fighting them, just allow them to be there. Observe them and smile to yourself at your new perception of them. I tend to find that acknowledging them with a kind of 'yeah, yeah' works well! They are only thoughts in your head and if you treat them like this they won't affect your body hitting the ball.

As you were reminded in the last chapter, you are playing golf for fun, so be sure to 'play.' Rather than trying to remember everything about how to swing the club, spend more time just hitting the ball the way you want to! This will introduce more freedom and fluidity into your swing and you'll certainly enjoy it more.

It can help to see your body as a powerful golf club swinging machine. Once you've programmed it and pressed the start button you want to get out of the way. Otherwise you're going to jam up the mechanism and it's not going to be pretty! Realise that your unconscious is far better at controlling the club than your conscious mind. Take putting for example. Many people struggle as they try to work out how hard to hit the ball.

So stop trying to work it out mentally. Say to yourself "I trust that my unconscious mind knows how hard to this" and let go. Practice this for a while and notice that when you over hit or under hit a putt, it's because you were trying to consciously work out the distance and you were physically tighter. With practice you'll learn to trust your unconscious mind more and more, and you'll hole a lot more putts.

Putting it all together

This chapter covers how you can apply all of the physical and mental tips in this book, which require some conscious thought, with an unconscious approach to hitting the ball.

Put very simply you develop a pre-shot routine that breaks each shot into two parts:

1. Mental (conscious)
2. Physical (unconscious)

Then you keep it separate. Trying to be aware of all the different stages of your swing would be like consciously working out how to elegantly leap out of the way of a speeding bus at the last second. You can't do it.

So here is what I recommend:

Build up your winner's mindset before you get to the course and think about it between shots.

When it comes to your shot stick to the following 2 part routine.

1. The Mental Part of your shot:

   - Stand in a confident way, take a decision about the shot and commit to it 100%

   - Take out the club you've chosen, but don't stand over the ball yet

   - Choose the exact spot where you want the ball to go*

   - Remember the best shot you've ever hit with the same club and address the ball

   - See the whole shot you're about to hit in full including the landing or the putt rolling into the hole at the appropriate speed – faster for an uphill putt, and slower for a downhill one. (You're showing your unconscious the shot you want it to hit.)

*When you're choosing the spot, remember to be accurate. For example, if you're putting, don't say to yourself 'left edge of the hole', unless you want the ball to finish on the left edge of the hole. I tend to find it helps to repeat mantras in my head, such as "Straight down the middle" or "In the hole." This keeps your conscious occupied and helps to make the message to your body very clear.

You've now programmed your unconscious and it's time to allow it to do its job, without you thinking you can do it better consciously.

Once you have gone through the Mental Part, don't delay. You want to minimise the time for uncertainty or talking yourself out of shot. Besides there shouldn't be anything to decide. If you are feeling unsure then you haven't gotten yourself into a confident state at the start. Step back from the ball, begin again and commit completely to the shot you want to hit.

The Physical Part of the shot:

- Take the positive feeling from the best shot you've hit, but don't worry about how this shot will turn out. Let go of the outcome and give your attention to the doing rather than the result. Remind yourself that you need to trust your unconscious and allow it to hit the ball.

- Take a deep 'ha' breath in and out and swing in a way that feels good.

How this applies to your life

Most of us have experienced times when we over think things. We try to become so consciously clear about what we are doing that we either end up feeling confused or overwhelmed. Our performance suffers or we decide not to take any action at all.

It can help to form a similar two step strategy for things you want to achieve in life. You could see it as: Planning and Taking Action.

1. Planning
- Get yourself into a confident state
- Decide what you want to achieve
- Imagine how you want it to happen
- Keep your focus on what you want to happen (rather than on what could go wrong)

2. Taking Action
- Take the first step. (Don't worry about future steps until you get to them)
- Instead give your attention to what you are doing

Practicing

Don't be crazy!

Be flexible when you're trying to improve. Don't just practice the same shot harder if you aren't getting results; instead really change what you do.

Hard work and practice certainly play an important part, but it's not always about trying harder, unless you do it smarter too. Trying the same behaviour hoping for new result is insane!

How this applies to your life

If there is a situation that you are unhappy with, then make a change. Don't just wait for something miraculous to happen; try something new. In a dispute, don't just push back harder; change your approach. Over 90% of our thoughts are the same today as they were yesterday. Look for books and courses to expand your mind to get some new ideas! What can you do differently to change a situation?

Review what you've learned

This book is designed so that it's easy to review what you've learned. Keep referring to it regularly, and notice your all round progress, not just in the better scores you'll get. I don't know how quickly things will improve for you, but I do know that the tips in this book will improve your golf game and your life. There is one condition: you need to practise what you have learned regularly in order to get the hang of it. Stick with it and the results will come. I hope you do and I look forward to hearing about your success!

About the author

Ed McCosh is a Confidence Coach, getting great results internationally. He works with golfers to improve their mental game and scores, and he hel s people to feel calmer about life in general too.

For more information on how Ed will help you further improve your golf game & your life through seminars and personal coaching go to:

www.edmccoshconfidencecoach.com

Here are some of the unique things you'll get when you work with Ed:

- Let go of limiting beliefs & negative emotions (like anger, fear, guilt & sadness)

- Get over what holds you back from getting what you want!

- Change how you feel about certain clubs

- More physical techniques to stop wasting nervous energy before a round

Other books also available by Ed McCosh:

"Am I good enough?"

The ultimate guide to overcoming your fears and raising your confidence.

"Letting go of anger"

How to live a calmer, healthier and happier life.

For more information go to:

www.edmccoshconfidencecoach.com

How to improve your golf game (and your life!)